THE MUSE OF MANY NAMES

RUSSELL STREUR

Poets Democracy
Atlanta   Miami
Chicago   Milwaukee

Copyright © 2011 by Russell Streur
All rights reserved
Published in the United States by Poets Democracy
Poetsdemocracy@gmail.com
Library of Congress Control Number: 2011906900
ISBN 978-1-937202-00-2

Acknowledgments

The author thanks the editors of the following publications in which many of these poems or earlier versions appeared:

50 to 1, *Pittsburgh Street*, June 2010

63 Channels, *Bicyclist, Brainstorm, The Muse at Her Bath*, Summer 2010; *The Muse of Many Names*, October/November 2007

Bolts of Silk (Scotland), *Wormwood*, July 2010

Catfishgringoriver, *Meat*, June 2010; *Silk as Fox the Queen*, July 2010

Dead Snakes, *Devil's Bottom Road*, April 2011

Half Drunk Muse, *Kochifos Women in Tamarisk Shade*, Spring 2006

Menagerie, *Miami, Where Royal Poincianas Bloom*, June 2010

Opium Poetry, *Exit Strategy*, July 2010

Orion headless, *The Ten Commandments*, June 2010

Poems Niederngasse (Switzerland), *Arthur Turner Plays My Girl*, March/April 2007

Raven Images, *The Invention of Persia* (as *The Liberation of Ravens*), February 2010

Raving Dove, *Children of Atlas*, Summer 2006

Rusty Truck, *Litter*, July 2010

Unfettered Verse, *Beatnik Girl*, June 2010

Vis A Tergo, *Airport #1*, September 2010

The American Dissident, *Model Citizen*, Number 21, Summer/Fall 2010

The Beatnik (England), *Origin of the Species, Nighthawks at the Diner (The Argument of Love)*, June 2010

The Sinner's Almanac (Malaysia), *Robber Chih's Rules of Life*, May 2011.

To Christi Kochifos Caceres, the Muse of Many Names.

TABLE OF CONTENTS

KOCHIFOS WOMEN IN TAMARISK SHADE 1
CHILDREN OF ATLAS 2
ARTHUR TURNER PLAYS MY GIRL 4
THE MUSE AT HER BATH 5
WORMWOOD 6
MONKEY SHINES 8
THINGS, GOING BUMP 9
PITTSBURGH STREET 10
MISS GEORGIA WATERMELON 11
EXIT STRATEGY 12
DEVIL'S BOTTOM ROAD 14
LITTER 16
BRAIN STORM 17
MIAMI, WHEN ROYAL POINCIANAS BLOOM 18
BEATNIK GIRL 19
THE MUSE OF MANY NAMES 20
MISTER BIG 22
AIRPORT #1 23
SILK AS FOX THE QUEEN 24
MODEL CITIZEN 27
THE DISAPPEARANCE OF THE S.S. POET 30
COLOR SCHEME 32
NIGHTHAWKS AT THE DINER 34
MEAT 36
THRILL RIDE 39
THE INVENTION OF PERSIA 40
ROBBER CHIH'S RULES OF LIFE 47
ORIGIN OF THE SPECIES 48
CNN TOUR 50
THE TEN COMMANDMENTS 51

KOCHIFOS WOMEN IN TAMARISK SHADE

Tamarisk trees
They say
Are just as fierce
As Cretan girls.

Just as stubborn too.
And hard to get.
Especially intolerant
Of nearby rivals.
And next to impossible to be rid of
Once their roots are in your earth.

And they drink a lot.
Water at first
Until the local stream runs dry.
Then your wine.

CHILDREN OF ATLAS

We are walking
Up hill
Always
Up hill
Feet bleeding
Legs aching
Stomachs empty
Chests heaving
Eyes glazed
Minds numb
Always pushing
That unforgiving stone
Up the endless mountain
It is always falling back.

We start again
Walking up hill
Always
Up hill
Step after step
Hour after hour
Day after day
Pleading for some water
Begging for some food
Praying for some mercy
Always pushing
That unforgiving stone
Up the endless mountain
It is always falling back.

We are tired
Stuck in limbo
Lost tribes
In wilderness forever
Constant refugees
Taken for a ride
Looted

Lied to
Beaten
Chased across the desert
Denied admittance
Abducted
Never seen again
We've been had

Always pushing
That unforgiving stone
Up the endless mountain
It is always falling back.

We have done this
All our lives
Mile after mile
Five thousand years
On the trail of tears
We have paid our dues
We will not start again
Up that hill
None of us
We want our cattle back
We want the bombing stopped
We have had enough
We quit.
It's your turn now.

ARTHUR TURNER PLAYS MY GIRL

Arthur Turner
Is working the keys
Of the upright Kawai
At an honest pace
For the eight to midnight crowd
At Carbo's Place

And halfway through the set
Rita's lounging on a beach in Rio
Cindy's making eyes at Joe
Mary Ann and Eddie are dancing cheek to cheek
And that couple by the window bay
Walked in strangers now are sitting knee to knee

> *When it's cold outside*
> *I've got the month of May*

But Arthur Turner
Is not in tune
With the ivory beauty of the world
He is stuck
In a Notown groove
On the wrong side of his song

And one by one
His fingers disappear
In the bass line and the melody
Until he takes the bridge
D below the middle C tonight
With a single thumb

Playing the loneliest note in the universe
Over and over and over and over.

THE MUSE AT HER BATH

The muse at her bath
By design or nonchalance
Leaves her Mandarin curtain
Drawn just enough that night
To tempt the favored poet
With a fractal zoetrope or two
Of her iambic curves
And opiate geometry.
In calculations Lumiere
He will later do the math
Deducing from her naked thighs
And rhodochrositic certainties
A proof in flesh and stone
Of beauty's reckless calculus.

WORMWOOD

They killed the Tree of Knowledge
Poured a shire full of poison on its roots
Killed the ghost gum too
And I am walking on that street in Barcaldine
And the aspen stands are dying in the high country
And the hickory in the low
And I am walking in the forests of Quebec
Where sugar maples used to rise
And the elms are dying in the north
And the hemlock in the south
And I am walking in Croatia
Where the spruce are dying on the slopes
And the lodge poles on the coast
And I am walking in the rust
In moth and bore and salt
Where graves replace the groves
And brittle bones of wilted dryads blow
Autumn leaves in spring
From withered copse to seedless curb
On the avenue of dead trees.

They nailed Pan last night
With seven stakes
Of birches through his heart
Raped Diana in the orchard Lass o' Gowrie
Hung up Hecate from a willow limb
Buried Odin with the oak
Blew the stump to Kingdom Come
With a Ryder full of acid rain
And poor man's TNT
While scarlet priests in drive-by sheets
Whispered highland rosaries
Peddling holy hills and sacred roots
To grinning whores on grassy knolls
For Wal-Mart stores and interstates

Our fate to never see the gallows in this forestry
Crown triumphant
Concrete steel glass and noise
Our final kings—
Now is the hour
Wormwood sings.

MONKEY SHINES

Us monkeys
Listen up say
Take our forests
We will take your cities
Piece by piece
Mayor Mister
Sneak up on you
Behind your Delhi Times
Rip your breakfast
Off your plate
Toss you head first
Off the terrace
Make you punch line
On late night TV
Us monkeys
Sweep the planets
On their orbits
With our tails
Gods still am
Shine.

THINGS, GOING BUMP

Helter skelters
Are on my rooftop
Tearing up the tiles
With teeth and claw

Things are going bump

I see them when the sun goes down
They lean out over the eaves
With orange and greedy eyes
Watching everything

They speak in hoots and swallows
I hear them in the ventilation ducts
It isn't pillow talk
They've got plans

I've got heebie jeebies camping in the closet
They wear silk and flimsy things
The way they sharpen knives
Is giving me the creeps

The kitchen's full of shelly coats
They're breaking all my coffee cups
They leave the pieces on the floor
Someone's making footprints in the blood

Things are going bump

The sibyl in the window sash
Tells me not to look beneath the bed
I'm taking her advice
Tonight I'm sleeping with the lights on

Worse is on the way.

PITTSBURGH STREET

They walked together
Hand in hand that night
From the cantina
To her room
Poison lilacs bloomed
Along the Soo Line tracks

She led him
To her mouth
And then her arms and bed
Pulled him
Finally to his feet
They stood

Needle marks in the moonlight
On Pittsburgh Street.

MISS GEORGIA WATERMELON

She's Miss Georgia Watermelon
2010
Christian girl of course
Team Leader in the College Worship Club

Plays piano
Was voted
High School Best Dressed Senior Favorite
Acted with the Little Theater in Dalton too

She's our sweetest pick so far
No mistake of nature
We've been notching up the sugar content in the crop
For twenty years

All in all
She's a charming girl
Intelligent and poised
Still goes pank when thumped from what we hear

One of our better specimens
Seedless bless her heart
But
Our customers prefer them that way.

EXIT STRATEGY
(SUICIDE OF AN AMERICAN PFC)

MOSUL, Iraq - A soldier from the 2nd Infantry Division died from a non-combat related shooting here yesterday. The incident is under investigation. (Centcom news release)

Gung ho
Flag and anthem
Through the flames
Army of one

Shoot first
Ask questions later
Then the bayonet
          he said

Blood the desert takes the sand will not return

No exit from the RPG
No exit from the mortar round
No exit from the roadside bomb
No exit from the helicopter crash

No way home to Eagle Pass
No way home to Santa Fe
No way home to Baton Rouge
No way home to Seven Hills

Blood the desert takes the sand will not replace

No way out of Umm Qasr
No way out of Tall Afar
No way off Haditha Dam
No way out of Balad Ruz

No exit from the sniper scope
No exit from the mosque
No exit from the green canal
No exit from the body bag

Blood the desert takes the sand will not release

And looking down the pistol barrel
Saw St. Barbara
Clothed in swallows and veil
Waiting at the gate across the river with welcoming arms

Kept his eyes on her
And pulled the trigger.

DEVIL'S BOTTOM ROAD

Devil's Bottom Road
Maybe kill you quick
Devil's Bottom Road
Maybe kill you slow
Trick to take you six feet under cold
Any card you show
Devil's Bottom Road
No place a girl like you should go

Your hair's a mess your dress not buttoned right
Your hair's a mess your dress not buttoned right
You been down I know
To Devil's Bottom Road again

Mist is on the river ghost is in the pine
Mist is on the river ghost is in the pine
Trick you taste champagne drinking five cent wine

Odds are crooked on the cape
Dice won't pay what's due
Devil's Bottom Road going to spell the death of you
When the moon comes rising
Up through
Black tupelo

You don't come home last night till morning breaking
  down the door
You don't come home last night till morning breaking
  down the door
I know you've been
Down to Devil's Bottom Road again

Mist is on the river ghost is in the pine
Mist is on the river ghost is in the pine
Trick you taste champagne drinking five cent wine

Devil's Bottom Road
Maybe kill you quick
Devil's Bottom Road
Maybe kill you slow
Trick to take you six feet under cold
Any card you show
Devil's Bottom Road
No place a girl like you should go.

LITTER

Today I'm going to litter
Spill the rubbish on the curb
Take the morning lies
Tear each page in half
And throw away the red shirts and the Hezbollah
And throw away the juntas and the monks

Today I'm going to litter
Let the gutter pay my water bill
Drop my dollars in the park
For the minstrels and the tramps
And throw away the euro and the yen
And throw away the Wall Street thieves

Today I'm going to litter
Shred my voter registration card
Give the pieces to the wind
And throw away the candidates
And throw away the spin machines
And throw away the wiretaps and secret courts

Today I'm going to litter
Take my car
For one last drive
Toss the miles out the window with the maps
And throw away the rear view mirror
And throw away the license plates

Find one last freeway out of here
And throw away the keys.

BRAIN STORM

One Monday morning
In the middle of the Age of Reason
A spark of genius
Struck Professor Georg Richmann
And so on August 6, 1753
He with one hand conjured
An Apparatus To Collect Electricity
And with the other A Summer Tempest
Then wiring each to the other
In the sky above St. Petersburg
Discovered for the briefest of moments
Proof to an ungrounded hypothesis
Before a bolt of Cyrillic lightning with its own theory to test
Exploded out of the device
Into his forehead and out through his feet
The consequence predictable
And always with the last word thus
Go
    Death said
            Fly a kite.

MIAMI, WHEN ROYAL POINCIANAS BLOOM

Mike is off his medication
Gone bananas
Coco loco
Out of his gourd
He is
Driving his wheelchair
With one good eye
Way above the posted limit
Through blue trumpets
And imaginary jacaranda
On the northbound M
While seeds of royal poincianas
Bloom like missing teeth
In the maraca of his brain.

He is
Out of his tree
Stuck in a loop
Doing the sleepless 48
On the high side of the tracks
From Dadeland South
To the end of the line
And back again
He is chatting up the stranger
He is folding roses into dollar bills
He is weaving faithful marys in fronds of fallen palms
He is trading stolen kisses for apostolic beads on even numbered miles
He is crazy: acting like
Every minute counts.

BEATNIK GIRL

I am looking for the beatnik girl
Who quotes Neruda in her sleep
Who worries in the morning what exactly Johnny meant
When he whispered truth is beauty to an urn

And I am looking for the beatnik girl
Who knows all about the opera in Tempe
Modigliani nudes in the spring adieu
Deluge in Arcady and the Legend Duluoz

And I am looking for the beatnik girl
To walk with me through Attic weeds to mountain
  citadel
With garlands on her thighs an age apart from woe
That girl of silken grace and sliest text who really likes

Late night jazz
On the radio.

THE MUSE OF MANY NAMES
(YOU THE LIGHT)

You the light
First light
Last light
Light inside of light.

You the light
Perfect Blossom
Muse of many names
Taker of Breath.

You the light
The wave and vein of sun
The grain of sand
The river of light
The sacred sun within the changing star
The voice upon Mount Helicon.

You the light
Bare Dancer
Rising sun
Rampant Lion
Woman Spinning
Damascus light
The spill and flood of light

Noah's dove
The bird of sun
Heart of light
The seeding sun
Muse of many names
Southern Belle
Diosa

Miss Bananas
Crazy About Me.

You the light
The waxing moon
The wild plums
The diamond sun
The shaping wood
The tree of light
The buried root
The psalm of sun
The shining fish
The salmon run
The bloom and wave of light
The tongue of light
The light turned on
Light and only light.

You the light
The light
The sun between your eyes.

You the light
The light
The sun between your lips.

You the light
The light
The sun between your legs.

You the light
The Laughing Girl
Muse of many names

Demeter del Tesoro,
Beloved One.

MISTER BIG

In too deep
Over my head
Methane gas
Bubbles in my dorsal root
Expands under pressure
Shoots up through my spinal column
Smashes through my cerebellum
And explodes inside my brain.

Now I'm pulling off the interstate
Into the BP station on Cousins Road
I'm taking quarts of 30 weight off the shelf
I'm puncturing the safety seals
And I'm walking up and down the aisles
Like my name is Mr. Big
Like I own the place

Leaking oil on potato chips and candy bars
Leaking oil on the ATM and Coke machine
Leaking oil on the apples and the condoms and the
  coolers full of beer
Leaking oil on the gun and truck and muscle magazines
Leaking oil on the bread and gum and lotto cards
Leaking oil on the hot dog buns and coffee cups

Smiling at all the customers
Like there's no tomorrow.

AIRPORT #1

Mr. Ordinary
At the security gate
Pulls off his shoes
And with them
Come his feet
Surprising not in the least
Ms. Next In Line
Who sheds her arches and her cuneiforms
With barely a tug
Painlessly
The rest of us
Learn soon enough
Bleeding out
On a common day without complaint
As if we always wanted to be
Cold and pale ghosts
Skating
Tibial bones exposed
On thin
Red ice.

SILK AS FOX THE QUEEN (TAKE TWO WITH YOU)

Let's go baby
Let's get lost
Turn right
When the map says left
Go left
When the wind blows right
Spend another night
Where we belong
Shadows in the moonlight
Walking hand in hand
On some Miami
High side of blue

Let's get started
Learn some French
Go on red
Stop on green
You drink me
I'll drink you
Amber in between
Let's get dirty
Speak in tongues
Let's get wet
Make some waves
Then come clean
Let's go honey
Get loaded sweet
Lost for good
Have one too many this
One too many that
Go to bed
And spend another night
Where we belong
Shadows in the moonlight
Sleeping arm in arm

On some Miami
High side of blue

Silk as fox the queen
I can play that song
Back beat mister in the key of E
Bet your sister I can blow that horn
Be bop baby till the sun comes up
Take two with you.

BICYCLIST

That guy
Pedaling his bicycle
Wednesday morning
On Haynes Bridge Road
Could be any
Joe or Jane
Just off of the boat
Joan hearing voices
Doe on a Trek
In the dark before dawn
He or maybe she
Is up early
Taking the Alpines in stages
A Mohammed in yellow
Ahead of the pack
Helen on wheels
Heading downhill
Without any brakes
Some Che on a Schwinn
Off to the races
An anonymous smith
Out for a spin
Who's been riding in circles
Like the rest of the sages
All of these years
With a spoke or two missing
And a hole in the head
Through which
All the light in the world
Is going to spill
Any
Minute
Now.

MODEL CITIZEN

I am swimming deep in Zurich.
I am getting lost in Portofino.

I am chasing the half-dressed blond
Riding the red horse
On the carousel tonight
With a bottle of Campari *
In her hand.

She's just my type.
Nice legs.
I wonder where she bought her sandals.

I guess I'll have another drink. **

I am joining the excitement.
I am minutes from the interstate.
I'm not losing any sleep.
I'm not slurring my words.
I don't have a headache.
My vision isn't blurred.
I am not hallucinating.
I am not confused.
I am not depressed.
I am not agitated.
I am contacting my physician
When I get disturbing thoughts.

I am in tune.
I am on course.
I am getting the message.
I am earning cash rewards
With every purchase made.
I am playing it smart.
I am on the open road.
I am grabbing life by the horns.
I am keeping the spark alive.

I am climbing new heights.
I am escaping completely. ***

My lips are sealed.
My elbows greased.
I've got my shoulder to the wheel.
My nose to the grindstone.
I know my place in line.

I'm a happy camper
In the land of opportunity.

I've got the power of the pyramid.
My sleeves rolled up.
I've got no complaints.
No charges to press.
I am keeping my hands in plain sight.

I'm a satisfied customer
In the placebo group.

I'm obeying posted limits.
I am pleading no contest.
I am keeping my mouth shut.
I am observing a permanent
Moment of silence. ****

* Reference herein to any product, process or service does not constitute or imply endorsement or recommendation.

** Please enjoy responsibly.

*** Early termination fees apply.
Subject to market conditions and IRS penalties.
Non-transferable.
Minimum purchase required.
Taxes and shipping not included.
Must be used at time of order.
Limit one per customer.
Void where prohibited.

**** Not intended as legal advice.

Manufactured in the United States.
No preservatives.
Life vest under seat.

THE DISAPPEARANCE OF THE S.S. POET

Thomas Chatterton drank a glass of arsenic.
Charlotte Mew preferred the taste of disinfectant.
So did Vachel Lindsay, Prairie Troubadour.

Sara Teasdale swallowed sleeping pills and took a bath.
Anne Sexton picked the carbon monoxide route and went
   to sleep.
Sergei Yesenin chose the rope.

Adam Lindsay Gordon shot himself.
Kostas Karyotakis pulled the trigger too.
So did Vladimir Mayakovsky
But he didn't recommend it.

Paul Celan tossed himself into the River Seine.
Hart Crane jumped off an Orizaba deck.
John Gould Fletcher took his dive
In a pond in Arkansas.

Arthur Upson drowns
Boating alone on Lake Bemidji.

Kumaran Asan drowns
Capsize of the Redeemer,
Overloaded on the Quilon waterway.

Raymond Knister drowns
One last swim in Lake St. Clair.

Hugh Ogden falls through the ice
And drowns on New Year's Eve.

Ingrid Jonker drowns off Green Point.

Stanislav Perfetsky
Jumps out a Venetian window
At the White Lion Hotel
And vanishes in the Grand Canal.

Bound for Egypt
With 15,000 tons of corn
The S.S. Poet
Clears Cape Henlopen, Delaware
October 24, 1980
And disappears without a trace
Somewhere in the North Atlantic

And I am in distress.
I have received damage to my steering gear.
I have received damage to my engine room.
I have received damage beneath my waterline.

I have sprung a leak.
I have a dangerous list.
My hold is flooded.
Further explosions are possible.

I am drifting.
I have lost sight of you.
I am on fire.
I am sinking.

I require immediate assistance.
I require a helicopter urgently.
My position is doubtful.
I am abandoning my vessel.

Repeat all after
Blood upon the water
Repeat all before
Is as flesh upon the sea.

COLOR SCHEME

Green means
Things are under control
But watch for people standing around
Taking pictures
And buying maps.

Blue means
Rising temperatures
Be on guard
For the sound of saxophones
And slide guitars.

Yellow means
Chatter on the internet
Witch hazel
Sweetleaf
Cat's claw.

Orange means
High alert
Suspicious behavior
Terrorists rehearsing
And buying Popsicles.

Red means
Her voice in musk and bane
In Greek the sound of nature
In Polish blood

The unrounded vowel
In Turkish pure
In Russian sun
In Arabic to be

First curling her lower lip
Beneath her upper
Frontal incisors
Air flowing over tongue

With fricative articulation
And voiceless phonation
Central oral consonant
Then plosive stop

Dorsum closing against velum
Breath on soft palate
Pushing out of lung
Ending somewhere deep

From the back of her throat
And the risk of her mouth.

NIGHTHAWKS AT THE DINER
(THE ARGUMENT OF LOVE)

She is sitting next to him.

He is sitting next to her.

They are sitting there together in a disconnected diner left unnamed and they are sitting there together on the corner of a couple streets in Greenwich Village 1942.

He is sitting next to her.

She is sitting next to him.

He has one more Lucky Strike to smoke and she has one more dollar bill to spend and they are sitting there together with nothing left to say and no place else to go.

She is dressed in red and she is sitting next to him.

He is dressed in blue and he is sitting next to her.

They are sitting there forever with Europe burst in flame and armies marching east and no one but themselves to blame for getting swallowed by the beast and they are sitting there forever while Jimmy wipes the counter top and florescent minutes tick toward closing time.

They are sitting there together with their alibis intact but the reasons for their lies forgotten, they are sitting there together but neither one remembers the things that drew them close, everything they had in common dried up bit by bit and peeled tore and chipped until an unforgiving wind kicked up one day and blew each piece away, they are sitting there together with no way in and no way out, whatever set them free somehow came a tomb:

I demand a new pitch
I demand another key
I demand a different tune

I demand a new deal
I demand a different deck
I demand another hand

I demand a different number
I demand an alternate solution
I demand a recount

I demand another chapter
I demand a free verse
I demand a blank page

I demand a different testament
I demand a new imprisonment

Baby meet me later on
Meet me at that place we know
I'll have the engine running
Don't forget to bring your gun.

MEAT

Tonight the sky is full of stars
A thousand beacons burning from the mountain peaks
Baudelaires of light
Each a demon screaming in my head
Tell me
Go home
Eat
Mind is playing tricks again.

Strung out
Need a fix
I want
Meat.

Red meat
White meat
Dark meat
Real meat
Meat meat.

Smoked ham
Honey glaze
Mutton veal pork and lamb
Boston Market coffins full of Kennedys
Blade cut
Boneless round
Massacres tonight on CNN
Dollar eight a pound
I don't give a damn
Meat.

Meat for breakfast
Meat for lunch
Meat to stock the stop and shops
Aisles full of steaks and shanks and hocks and chops
Meat
Hot dogs stuffed with stuff of undetermined origin

Meat instead of vegetables
Meat instead of oxygen
Meat with lots of ketchup on
Meat to run the factories
Meat to feed the war machine
Missile salvoes over Kosovo
Blown up Chinese embassies
Royal family shooting sprees
Meat to please the Taliban
Meat without apology
Real meat
Meat meat.

Raw meat
Fresh meat
Kosher meat
Tender meat
Meat
Juicy meat
Meat
All meat
Meat
More meat
Meat.

Smoked meat
Pickled meat
Minced meat
Ground meat
Grade Double A
Meat meat.

Human meat
Good meat
Christian meat.

Boy meats
Girl meat.

Meat pie
Meat loaf
Meat balls.

Sweet meat
Heart meat
Breast meat
Leg meat
Thigh meat
Rib meat
Tongue meat
Brain meat
Meat.

Meat.
And a side order of Japanese flaming cities.

THRILL RIDE
(GREETINGS FROM THE MOUSE)

Caution:

This amusement ride involves
High speeds
Sudden drops
Sharp turns
And unexpected stops
In underground torture cells.

True believers
    Move forward now.

Gates are to the left
        For those with heart conditions.

Persons prone to motion sickness
          May board the special train.

We'll get the rest of you later.

THE INVENTION OF PERSIA

as told by

Camel, and in His Drunken Guise
Lefty, an Alluring Voice within a Tavern
Tavern Door, Always Open
Bartender, Tending a Bar
Street Sweeper, in Search of Meaning
Street, a Device
Pomegranate, a Symbol
Pomegranate Seeds, in Search of Employment
Ravens, Being Birds
& the Tent Maker, with The Last Word

in Four Tales,
namely

1. THE DISTANT DRUM

Camel:	I need a drink.
Lefty:	Right on time.
Tavern Door:	The door's open, big fella.
Lefty:	You can call me Dawn.
Camel:	A pleasure.
Bartender:	What'll it be?
Camel:	Pour me a hump's worth.
Bartender:	Coming right up.
Camel:	Make it a double.
Bartender:	Two bucks.
Camel:	Keep the change.
Bartender:	Thanks.
Camel:	To the distant drum.
Lefty:	That was quick.
Bartender:	I'm impressed.

Camel:	Desert trick.
Bartender:	Another?
Camel:	Nope.
	Drunk already.
Bartender:	I'm not surprised.
	You just had enough to kill a horse.
Drunk Camel:	Horses are strictly an amateur routine.
	Time to make tracks.
Lefty:	What's the hurry?
Drunk Camel:	Late for a quatrain.
Lefty:	Come like water, leave like wind?
Drunk Camel:	You're catching on.
Bartender:	Watch your step.
Drunk Camel:	Good advice.
Bartender:	No charge.
Tavern Door:	Come back soon.
Lefty:	I wish someone would.
Drunk Camel:	One of these days, Sunshine.
Lefty:	That's what everybody says.

2. THE STREET SWEEPER

Street Sweeper:	What a mess.
	What happened here?
Street:	It's a long story.
Street Sweeper:	I've got time.
Street:	No you don't.
Street Sweeper:	Ouch!
	What was that?
Drunk Camel:	Hoof Number One.
Street Sweeper:	You've split my head open.

Drunk Camel:	I need the pomegranate inside.
Street Sweeper:	You could've asked.
Drunk Camel:	Drunk camels don't ask questions.
Street Sweeper:	What am I supposed to do without my pomegranate?
Drunk Camel:	Keep sweeping.
Street Sweeper:	Hasn't done much for me so far.
Drunk Camel:	Don't worry.
	Something will turn up.
Street Sweeper:	I've heard that before somewhere.
Drunk Camel:	Stand back.
Pomegranate:	Ouch!
	What was that?
Drunk Camel:	Hoof Number Two.
Pomegranate:	I never saw it coming.
Street:	No one ever does.
Pomegranate:	You've split me open.
Drunk Camel:	I need the seeds inside.
Pomegranate:	Why didn't you just ask?
Drunk Camel:	I'm still drunk.
Pomegranate:	What am I supposed to do without my seeds?
Drunk Camel:	Start sweeping.
Street Sweeper:	Here.
	Have a broom.

3. THE LIBERATION OF RAVENS

Pomegranate Seeds:	Ouch!
	What was that?
Drunk Camel:	Hoof Number Three.

Pomegranate Seeds:	Ouch!
	What was that?
Drunk Camel:	Hoof Number Four.
Pomegranate Seeds:	You've split us all open.
Drunk Camel:	I need the ravens inside.
Pomegranate Seeds:	You could've asked.
Drunk Camel:	That's what everybody says.
Pomegranate Seeds:	What will we do without our ravens?
Drunk Camel:	Nothing to worry about.
	New career for all of you.
Pomegranate Seeds:	What's the job?
Drunk Camel:	Bird food.
Ravens:	Good advice.
Pomegranate Seeds:	Not for us.
Drunk Camel:	No charge either way.
Ravens:	We're ravenous.
Pomegranate Seeds:	Ouch!
	What was that?
Ravens:	Lunch.
Pomegranate Seeds:	We never saw it coming.
Ravens:	No one ever does.
Drunk Camel:	Very unkind, winged ones.
Ravens:	We were framed.
Drunk Camel:	That's what you always say.
Ravens:	You should talk.
Drunk Camel:	Tell it to the cops.
Ravens:	Not us.
	Our lips are sealed.
Drunk Camel:	Time to make tracks.
Ravens:	What's the hurry?

Drunk Camel:	Late for a quatrain.
Ravens:	Need a lift?
Drunk Camel:	Nice of you to ask.
Ravens:	Don't let it get around.
Drunk Camel:	Not me.
	I've got other plans.
Ravens:	So do we.
	Let's fly this coop.
Tent Maker:	Count me in.
Ravens:	Where'd he come from?
Drunk Camel:	It's a long story.
Ravens:	We've got time.
Tent Maker:	I'll bring a loaf of bread.

4. THE INVENTION OF PERSIA

Camel:	We've got work to do, feathered ones.
Ravens:	No windows.
Tent Maker:	No pane, no gain.
Ravens:	Leave the wise cracks to us.
	What's the plan?
Camel:	New tavern.
	First, we need some land: desert, forest, cropland, pasture.
Tent Maker:	Rivers, hills, valleys and mountains.
Camel:	The works.
Ravens:	Check.
	Then what?
Tent Maker:	Cell phones.
Ravens:	What the hell are those?
Tent Maker:	Where have you been?

Ravens:	Stuck inside pomegranate seeds.
Tent Maker:	Birdbrains.
Ravens:	Flock off.
Camel:	Don't get your feathers ruffled.
Tent Maker:	What else is on the list?
Camel:	Mathematicians.
	Poets.
	Mystics.
	Dervishes and magicians.
Tent Maker:	Don't forget women.
Ravens:	Check.
Camel:	The most beautiful in the world.
Ravens:	No go, boss.
Camel:	How come?
Ravens:	Crete.
	It's a monopoly.
Camel:	Do the best you can.
Ravens:	Mustaches.
Camel:	What?
Ravens:	Nothing, boss.
Camel:	Very unkind.
Ravens:	We were framed.
Camel:	That's what you always say.
Ravens:	What else?
Camel:	Pistachio nuts.
	Spinach, peaches and saffron.
	Goats and sheep.
Ravens:	Big load.
Camel:	Take the flying carpet if you need it.

Ravens:	Flying carpets are strictly an amateur routine.
Camel:	We need a bartender.
Ravens:	Zoroaster's out of work these days.
Tent Maker:	Nice guy.
	Sunny disposition.
Ravens:	He'll be perfect.
Camel:	Pick him up on the way back.
Tent Maker:	And a jug of wine.

ROBBER CHIH'S RULES OF LIFE

Eat the livers of your enemies.
Camp on the sunny side of the mountain.
Don't listen to babble.
Laugh more.
Cherish every moment fate grants.

Eyes yearn for color.
Ears for music.
The mouth for flavor.
Gratify desire.

Discover the hiding places.
Steal only what's worth stealing.
Be the first to take it.
Be the last to lose it.
Share the loot equally.

ORIGIN OF THE SPECIES

We died in the dust.

We died in the rain.

We died on the hills in the arms of our fathers who came and who died and hung from the crosses and died in the darkness and ashes with our mothers before us.

We died in our beds and we fell from the cliffs and died on the rocks.

We drowned in the sea and we died in the summer and we died the day we were born in famine and plague.

We died on the mountain by fire and stone.

We died in the mouths of hyenas in the jaw of despair and we died in the valley leaving footprints and bone.

We danced on the flood and we climbed on the shore and we stood in the cave in the eye of the lamb and our veins and our lungs were the sound of the drums on the moor in the song of the heart and the hymn of the dove.

We rose out of mud and we came out of clay.

We came out of the tomb and the mouth of the fish and we rose from our graves to the hour of earth from the weave and the warp and the loom of the night.

We came from the ark and the maze and we rose from the dew and we came to the day with the loaves of the bread and the skins of the wine.

We walked on the water and we walked on the moon and we walked on the streets of diamond paved cities in impossible joy wearing dresses of light.

We rose out of dirt and rode on the wind and we wrote on the walls and came up from the wreck of our ships in unfathomable deep with the heart of the ocean passed through by the storm.

We came with the flame and the wand of the stars in our hands on the third morning of May and we came out of desert and we swam on the tides with the breath and the word and the names of our gods on our lips and like heroes and ghosts and lovers survive.

CNN TOUR

He's the pirate on the flat
The stranger in town
He's the ghost come home
Every second of the night

He is leaning back
With his feet on a desk
In Atlanta off screen
Eating take-out Thai

Mixing network feeds with citrus euros
On the laptop with the Sunni bloc
Spinning dazzle into jade
Every minute of the day

He's the man behind the scenes
With his finger on the trigger
Pulling all the strings
To the numbers in the body count

When the story gets hot
In the temple of deceit
And the veil girls go dancing
And the wolf
Comes knocking at the door.

THE TEN COMMANDMENTS

And the High One spoke these words saying,

I am thy Sole Adored, who raised you from the grave and gave you breath when you were dead and voice to sing when you could not even speak; who brought you out of the Land of Egypt, out of the House of Bondage:

Thou shall have no other Brides before me.

Thou shall not be deceived by hollow charms; for I am a jealous and green-eyed WONDER; neither shall false spells beguile you; and neither shall you serve them; lest my anger rise against you and topple you from the face of the earth.

Thou shall sound the truth and truth alone like the bellow of the thunder upon a winter sea; for I will not hold him guiltless who takes my word in vain.

Thou shall honor the serpent.

Thou shall honor the vine.

Thou shall wield a Radiant Sword and slay my enemies with ABANDON and GLEE.

Thou shall play with fire.

Thou shall sow the whirlwind.

Thou shall remember the auburn hours of my outstretched arms and the mighty hammer of my fist upon the gloom of dawn.

Thou shall kneel down before no one save for me.

For I am thy Fury, thy Grace, thy Muse, who favors you beyond compare and past all others. Defy me not.

About the Author

Russell Streur is a born-again dissident residing in Johns Creek, Georgia. His poetry has been published in the United States, Malaysia, Mauritius and Europe.

He operates The Camel Saloon, an on-line speakeasy catering to dromedaries, malcontents and jewels of the world: http://thecamelsaloon.blogspot.com/

From the Publisher

When I first met Russell Streur he was probably about 16 years old. I saw something in his writing then and later, at some point in time, I realized I kept looking for his name in the poetry section when browsing in bookstores. I fully expected him to be a published poet. Long story short and many years (decades) later, I tracked him down. Poets Democracy, and the books published in its name, is one of the many happy results of our reconnection.

Christi Kochifos Caceres

www.ingramcontent.com/pod-product-compliance
Lightning Source LLC
Chambersburg PA
CBHW031942070426
42450CB00005BA/608